Dear Lord JESUS

Why do I have to go to church?

WRITTEN BY:
JACQUELINE B. KOHLS

ILLUSTRATED BY:
HARRY AVEIRA

Dear Lord Jesus
Why do I have to go to church?

For copyright permission, school visits and book readings/signings,
email info@jacquelinebkohls.com

Illustrations by: Harry Aveira 2019
Graphic Designer: Praise Saflor
Edited by: Bobbie Hinman – fairybooklady@bestfairybooks.com
Project Manager: April Cox – Little Labradoodle Publishing
www.ll-publishing.com

First Edition Oct 2019

Library of Congress Cataloging-in-Publication Data

Names: Kohls, Jacqueline B., author. | Aveira, Harry, illustrator.
Title: Dear Lord Jesus why do I have to go to church? /
written by Jacqueline B. Kohls ; illustrated by Harry Aveira.
Description: Fort Jennings, OH: Jacqueline B. Kohls, 2019.
Identifiers: LCCN 2019914205 | ISBN 978-1-7340428-2-5 (Hardcover) |
978-1-7340428-0-1 (pbk.) | 978-1-7340428-1-8 (e-book)
Subjects: LCSH Christian children—Religious life—Juvenile fiction. | Christian children—Conduct of life--Juvenile
fiction. | God (Christianity)—Juvenile fiction. | CYAC Christian children--Fiction. | Christian children—Conduct of
life—Fiction. | God (Christianity)—Fiction. | BISAC JUVENILE FICTION / Religious / Christian / Values & Virtues
Classification: LCC PZ7.1 .K6745 De 2019 | DDC [E]--dc23

Library of Congress Control Number : 2019914205

ISBN: 978-1-7340428-2-5 (Hardcover)

Dedication

This book is dedicated to all of God's children - young and old who might need a little reminding on why we should go to church.

Also, to my family and friends for your love and support throughout this new journey in my life.

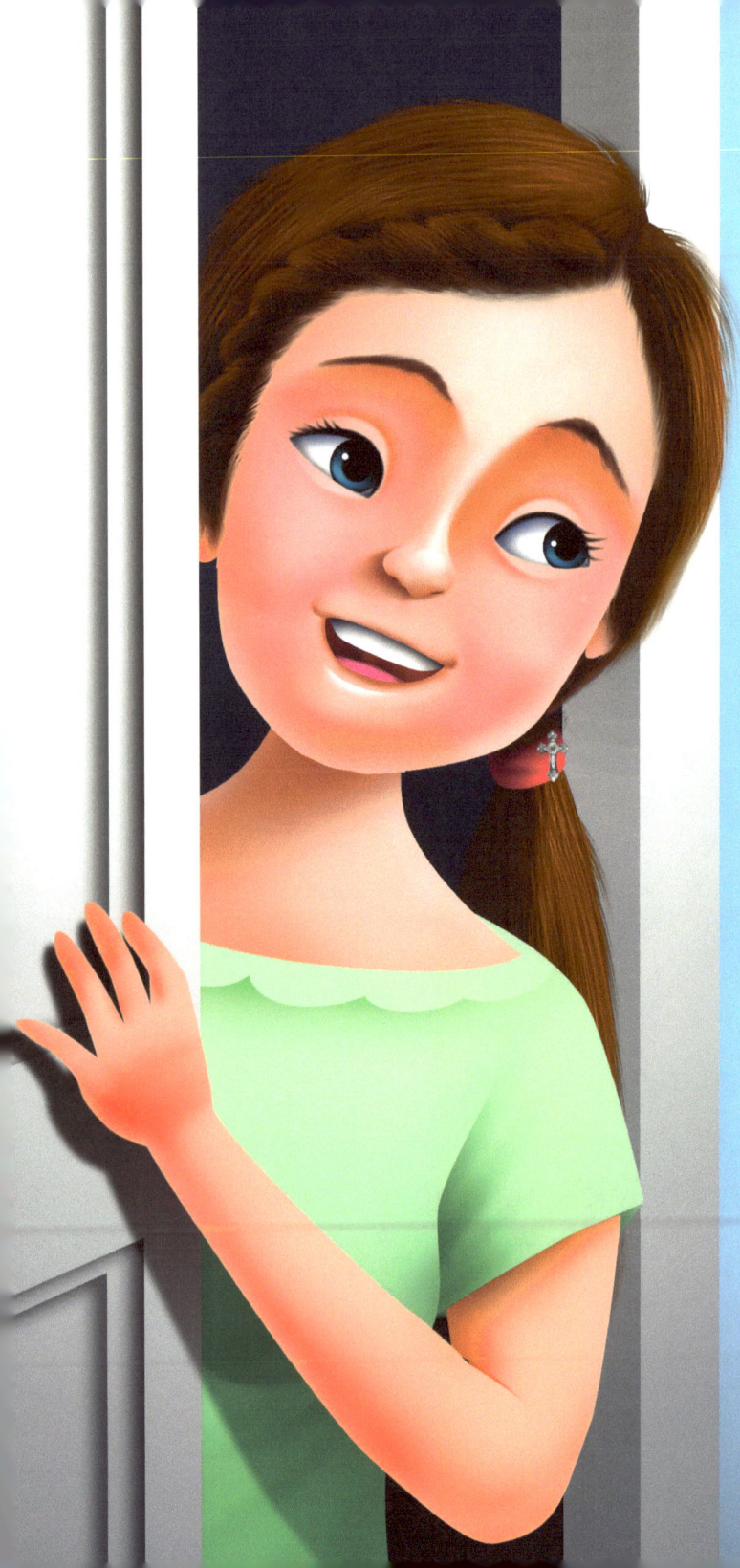

Dear Lord Jesus,

When I HEAR my mom say,
Time to start a new day!
If it's Sunday—I KNOW there
is more she will say.

Like, *Let's ALL go to church,*
thank our Lord up above.
Oh, No, NO, I say.
Staying in bed's what I love!

Can't we SKIP? I'm so tired.
Can't I wait 'til next week?
I don't want to get dressed,
plus I'm hungry and weak.

See, my mom has said things that are PROBABLY true,
But of course I just WANTED to run it by YOU.

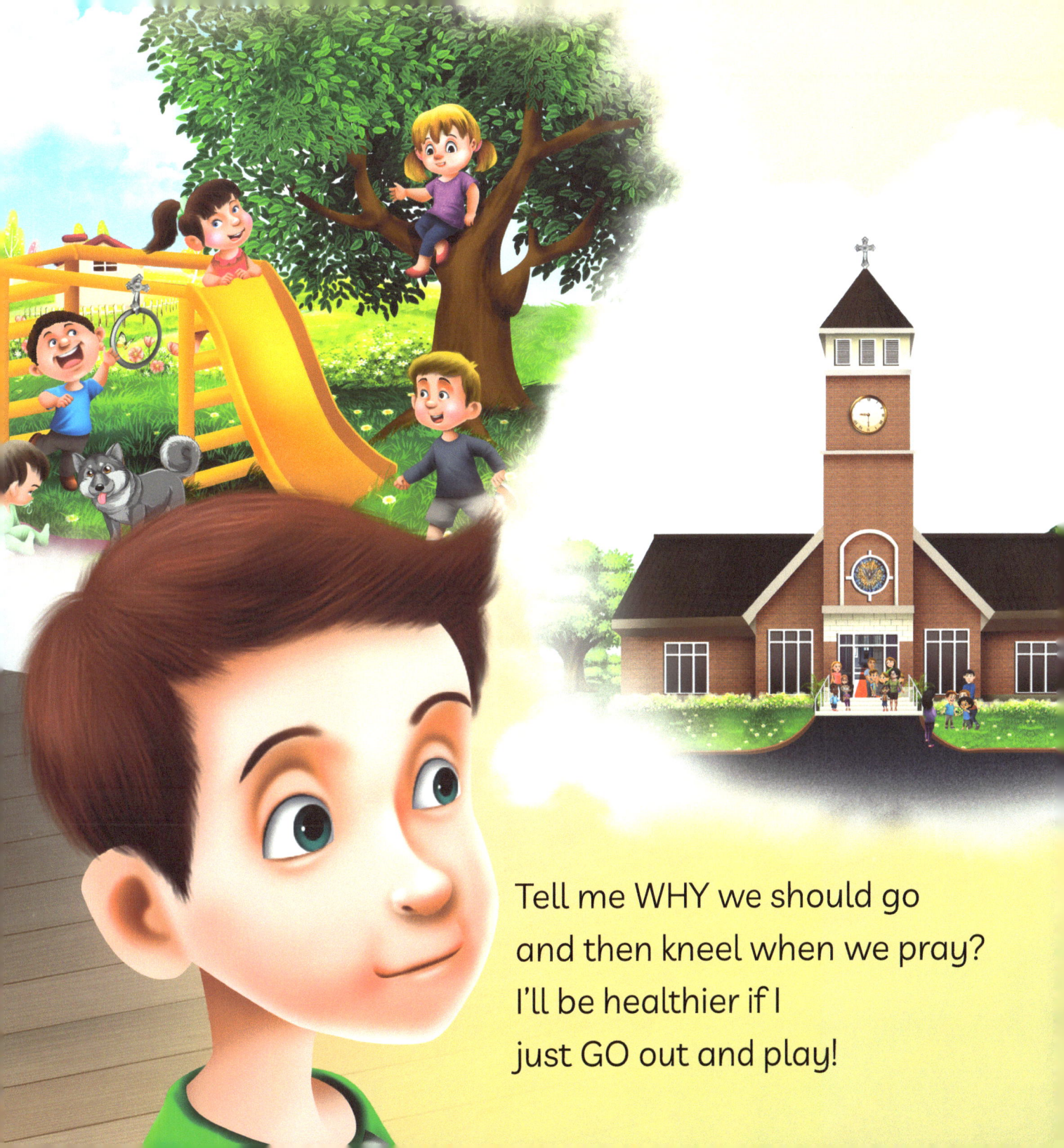

Tell me WHY we should go
and then kneel when we pray?
I'll be healthier if I
just GO out and play!

My mom SAYS you are with us from morning 'til night.

Even though we can't see you,
are we STILL in your sight?

When my Mom says we're
going to church just to pray,
Is it TRUE we are guests
in YOUR house,
and should stay?

But it's NOT like a party
with food and balloons.
Can I just stay at home?
Maybe watch my cartoons?

Is it TRUE when we pray and remember the cross,
The Holy Spirit surrounds us to help if we're lost?

And...if all this is true, then...

Tell me WHAT is this talk
about doing Communion?
This is making me dizzy
and causing confusion.

If it's TRUE you created
ALL things that grow,
Is there anything else
that we all need to know?

Your friend, Mason

Uh-oh...

What is THIS?

It's a letter from Lord Jesus himself!

And He says...

Get your Bible right down from the shelf.

Yes, I know you have questions
as most children do,
And I'll HELP to find
all the right answers for you.

Yes, Your mom is so right,
she is smart, she is wise.
God created the trees,
and the stars in the skies...

And the flowers that grow
and the rains that will fall.
For your family and others,
He created it all.

So the reason you come and you kneel and you pray,
Is to honor your Lord and give thanks every day.

And receiving Communion represents all my love.
It means bringing you closer to the Lord up above.

Your mom's right, I am with you each day and each night.
I am everywhere, always with you in my sight.

Every week as you come
to the church, you will find...
That you'll learn all the answers,
but one at a time.

I'll be happy to see
your bright face every week,
Watch you pray as you gather
the answers you seek.

From now on, every Sunday, be the first out of bed,

Then get dressed, brush your teeth and please tame that bed head.

Go to church, read your Bible, take some notes, bring a pen.
Bless The Father, The Son and The Holy Spirit. Amen.

Dear Lord Jesus

Thank you for my family. Watch over them I pray.

Thank you for my safety as I run and as I play.

Thank you for my teachers for teaching me so much.

Thank you for my friends and thank you for my lunch.

Thank you for my home and thank you for my bed.

Thank you for everything else
that might have been left unsaid.

Amen

"Let the little children come to Me, and do not hinder them, for the Kingdom of Heaven belongs to such as these"

Matthew 19:14

Dear Lord Jesus,

On a separate piece of paper, write a letter to Jesus.
What kind of questions would you want to ask him?
And then draw a picture to explain your questions.

Love your child,

Take some time to read over and ask a question or two each night to your child. Get to know what God and going to church really means to them.

Do you enjoy going to church every Sunday?	What was one thing that reminded you of God today?	Was there a lesson or moral of the story?
What could your church do different to make it more exciting for you to go?	What was this story about?	What kind of connection did you have with this story or the character?
What was one thing you learned from this story?	QUESTIONS	What are three things you thank God for everyday?
What was your favorite picture in the book? Explain why.	What is your favorite part about the story?	What was the problem in the story?
In the story, the author explained going to church every Sunday is like going to Jesus' birthday party. Would you be sad if no one came to your birthday party?	There was a few references to the Holy Spirit in the story. What does the Holy Spirit mean to you?	Why do you think the author gave the book this title?
What was the purpose of the author writing this story?	What was one thing you learned in church recently?	Are you tired and grouchy in the morning or happy and excited to get up and go to church?

Also, to make it exciting, read it again and see if they can find 3 hidden crosses(✝) on each page.

www.ingramcontent.com/pod-product-compliance
Lightning Source LLC
Chambersburg PA
CBHW042024090426

42811CB00016B/1729